MARK ROLLE

HIS ARCHITECTURAL LEGACY IN THE LOWER OTTER VALLEY

BY
ALAN FORD

The Otter Valley Association
Millennium Project
2001

The Mark Rolle Signature stone

CONTENTS

FOREWORD
By Lord Clinton

I have always been fascinated by the quantity, and especially the quality, of the Mark Rolle buildings on the Estate.

Alan Ford has painstakingly researched this excellent book to show how all this happened. We always knew, but had little record or plans of how it all came about.

The book gives an insight into the people concerned, and the dedicated hard work and perseverance required to carry this out. The buildings still provide a memorial in bricks and mortar, and they have stood the Test of Time.

The contributions of the owner, Mark Rolle, the Agent Lipscomb, and the Clerk of Works and Builder Robert Kingdom bring the text to life, and the excellent economic and social background behind farming puts the account of the construction of the Mark Rolle buildings in its place in history. The result is a book well worth reading, not only from the point of view of academic study, but also as an interesting account of those times.

I am most grateful to have this book on my bookshelf. It is one which readers who have an interest in the subject will pick up and read from time to time with satisfaction.

LORD CLINTON

INTRODUCTION

At the tender age of six, Mark George Kerr Trefusis inherited the vast Rolle Estates in North and South Devon. As Mark Rolle, he became one of the foremost benefactors in the county.

His benefactions were spread wide, but nowhere is their enduring legacy more evident than in the Lower Otter Valley, in the Parishes of Newton Poppleford, Colaton Raleigh, Otterton, East Budleigh with Bicton, and Budleigh Salterton.

The most significant imprint he left on the countryside lies in the farms he built, added to or altered, and the numerous cottages he provided. This is the principal subject of this book, set within its historical context.

To mark the new millennium, the Otter Valley Association decided to make a photographic record of the Mark Rolle buildings within its area, the heart of the Rolle Estate in South Devon. The project then expanded to include an exhibition of selected photographs, and this illustrated book.

The Association has been able to carry out this programme with the help of a Local Heritage Initiative Grant. The Local Heritage Initiative was developed by the Countryside Agency, and funded by the Heritage Lottery Fund and the Nationwide Building Society. We are most grateful to these sponsors.

I would also like to record my personal thanks to:

- Lord Clinton for contributing a Foreword to this book
- John Varley, Estates Director of the Clinton Devon Estates, for permission to consult the Rolle Estate Archive.
- all those who kindly permitted photographs to be taken of their properties, and especially those who allowed me to examine the inside of their cottages
- Gerald Millington, Honorary Archivist to the Rolle Estate, for directing me to sources, and for generously sharing his extensive knowledge with me
- Richard Coates whose intimate knowledge of buildings on the Estate was a great help

- Philip Greenhow for his comments and the loan of books now long out of print
- fellow members of the Built Environment Sub-Committee of the Otter Valley Association, Ken Jones, Don Papworth, Alan Ross, John Saul, Gordon Wilson and Nigel Wood, who collaborated in the photographic survey
- Brian Youngman whose search for buildings marked MR gave us a starting point for the survey
- Jed Falby for designing the layout of this book
- Brian Turnbull, who edited and typed the text, for his thoughtful suggestions and constant encouragement
- and, last but not least, to my wife, Lin, who accompanied me on most of my trips of exploration, and assisted greatly in my researches.

And now for a prudent disclaimer. A book of this length, hardly larger than an essay, can be no more than an introduction to this fascinating, complex story covering more than half a century. Avenues for further research open up in all directions. For errors of fact, I take full responsibility. I may too have interpreted the evidence, and drawn conclusions that will not be justified by further research. These are the inevitable pitfalls of writing a short account within strict time limits.

In conclusion, I must add that very many of the buildings covered by our survey still belong to Lord Clinton, in what is now the Clinton Devon Estate. It is a pleasure to record that they are well maintained and cared for, and continue to enrich the heritage of the Lower Otter Valley.

Alan S Ford MA, FRIBA.

The Hon. Mark Rolle - in his prime.

MARK ROLLE (1835 – 1907) AND THE ROLLE ESTATE

By the 19th century, the Rolle family were very substantial landowners, after centuries of acquisition by marriage or purchase. They held land in Somerset, Cornwall, and Ireland with smaller holdings elsewhere, but the vast bulk of their Estates was in Devon.

The Rolle Estate Act of 1865 refers to the Devon Estate as containing "upwards of Fifty five thousand Acres, of which Thirty thousand Acres are in North Devon and the Remainder thereof in South Devon". Bateman's "Great Landowners of Great Britain", published in 1883, records the Rolle Estate as the largest in Devon, and confirms that it ran to nearly 55,600 acres.

The North Devon Estate was centred on Stevenstone House, near Great Torrington, while the South Devon Estate was centred on Bicton House, near East Budleigh, with outlying properties at Beer.

Born in 1835, Mark Rolle came to inherit the Estate in a curious way. The direct male line of the Rolle family came to an end when John, 2nd Lord Rolle, died in 1842 without a surviving male heir. In his Will, Lord Rolle placed the Estate in the hands of four Trustees, one of whom was the 19th Baron Clinton. The trust was in favour of Baron Clinton's second son, the Hon. Mark George Keri Trefusis, to hold for his lifetime. On his death, the Estate would pass to Lord Clinton's third son, or this son's heir. The Estate was thereby entailed, and Mark was in fact tenant for life. But how did he become involved in the inheritance at all at the tender age of six?

Already in the 17th century, there were links by marriage between the Rolle and the Clinton/Trefusis families. Later, Lord Rolle took as his second wife Louisa Trefusis, sister to both the 18th and 19th Barons Clinton. Mark Trefusis was, therefore, her nephew.

A condition of Lord Rolle's Will was that Mark would take the name Rolle in place of his family name. In 1852, now aged sixteen and at Eton, he duly assumed the name and arms of Rolle in place of Trefusis by Royal Licence, and became the Hon. Mark Rolle. It should be noted, however, that he never held the title of Lord Rolle or, indeed, any other peerage.

During Mark Rolle's minority, the Trustees administered the Estate in his interest. Indeed, ever afterwards, the Trustees of Lord Rolle's Will were associated with the administration of the Estate even though Mark Rolle himself became the effective landlord and decision-maker, and the original Trustees died or were replaced.

In 1860, Mark Rolle married Gertrude Jane Douglas, daughter of the Earl of Morton by whom he had two daughters. Both daughters married but neither had children. A few years later, he and the Trustees applied to Parliament to vary the very strict terms of Lord Rolle's Will. The result was the Rolle Estate Act of July 1865, which runs to sixteen pages of legal exactitude and, for the layman, doubtful clarity. The main points, however, fall under two heads.

Firstly, the Will required Mark Rolle to spend every summer in residence at Stevenstone and Bicton. However, Lady Louisa, Lord John Rolle's widow, had already exercised the option to reside at Bicton offered to her by his Will, and this effectively prevented Mark Rolle living there. It may be also that he found his aunt rather daunting. An American visitor in 1868 described her as "a remarkable woman, without equal or like in England, in one vigorous well-developed individuality of will and genius. She is a female rival to Alexander the Great."

It was also pleaded on Mark Rolle's behalf that, as he "is of delicate constitution, and has been advised by a Physician of Eminence that, if possible, he ought not to reside permanently in Devonshire, especially during the summer", the residential conditions should be eased. This contention may astonish later generations of holidaymakers and retired folk!

In the event, the Act declared that it would be sufficient for him to reside for three months at any time of the year at Stevenstone during Lady Louisa's lifetime, and after her death, which occurred in 1885, at Bicton and Stevenstone in alternate years.

As this book is largely concerned with the Lower Otter Valley, it is interesting to note that Mark Rolle did not live there until after 1885, and then only for a few months at a time. It would seem that Stevenstone was always regarded as his principal seat. He rebuilt the old house there on such a lavish scale that it took four years to complete. He was buried at Huish Church on the North Devon Estate.

The second, and more significant, element of the Rolle Estate Act was the relaxation of a number of terms of Lord Rolle's Will to enable the Estate to be managed more efficiently and flexibly. Provision was made for accepting the surrender of certain types of lease, and for buying in leaseholds in exchange for annuities. Power was granted for the making of roads, sewers and watercourses.

Even after the passing of the Act, Mark Rolle was still very far from having absolute mastery. As the Estate was Settled Land, that is subject to an entail, the expenditure of capital, as distinct from income, was tightly controlled by the Court of Chancery. This was to ensure that the overall capital value of the Estate should not be diminished during Mark Rolle's tenancy for life. As will be seen, the Settled Land Act of 1882 only eased the situation to a limited extent.

Lord Rolle's Will, the resulting Trust, the entail and the Rolle Estate Act are complex matters, even when reduced as here to their essentials (without, it is hoped, too much inaccuracy). It is therefore a relief to turn to the comparative simplicities of his life and character.

A newspaper obituary at the time of his death described him as "one of those great landowners who recognize most fully that property has its duties as well as its rights, and his ample purse was never closed to any appeal, religious, patriotic, or philanthropic which commended itself to a singularly cool and temperate judgement."

Another notice says, "Mr Rolle was of a very retiring disposition. In person, he was known to comparatively few of the public in the county." But it goes on to state "To all on the Estates he was a personal friend, for he always made it a point of seeing anyone connected with the property who came to him, however humble the caller's position might be."

The papers made much of the delicate condition and ill health which led him to go abroad during the winter. Indeed, it was in the South of France that he died in April 1907. Even so, he had been keen on sport, particularly cricket and hunting. As a young man, he played cricket for Devonshire, and captained the county eleven for several years. He maintained a large pack of hounds at Stevenstone, largely at his own expense. He also had an abiding passion for horses and kept a stud of around twenty there.

As one of the obituary notices puts it, "the difficulty when one desires to refer to Mr Rolle's public benefactions is to know where to commence." A modest summary would have to include helping to fund the restoration of Exeter Cathedral and of many churches on his Estate, the building of churches at Beer and Budleigh Salterton, and the re-building of Holy Trinity, Exmouth. Also in Exmouth, he was chief contributor to the erection of the Jubilee Clock Tower, leased the Manor Gardens to the town (returning the rent each year), contributed to the formation of the Beach Gardens and paid for the upkeep of the Strand enclosure.

He was instrumental in the creation of the branch railway to Budleigh Salterton and its later continuation to Exmouth. He gave financial support to the Royal Devon and Exeter Hospital, and gave land for the Cottage Hospitals in Torrington and Budleigh Salterton. He was particularly generous to schools and, until the passing of the Education Act of 1902, was the principal contributor to the support of schools on his Estate, including those in East Budleigh, Budleigh Salterton, Otterton and Newton Poppleford. He constantly encouraged his tenants to help in their upkeep by paying the Voluntary School Rate.

Memorial stone at water point, East Budleigh.

Ever mindful of the needs of those living on his Estate, he laid on a piped water supply to East Budleigh and Colaton Raleigh largely at his own expense in 1887 in commemoration of Queen Victoria's Golden Jubilee. He also contributed to the improvement of the water supply in Otterton.

It was inevitable that someone in his position would take a part in public life. He was a Deputy Lieutenant for Devon, and in 1864 became High Sheriff of the County. At one time he was a captain in the North Devon Yeomanry, High Steward of Barnstaple and patron of thirteen parish church livings. Yet, he was not generally prominent in public affairs, which were no doubt unsuited to his "retiring disposition". Perhaps this explains why he was never granted a title.

His public persona was much more that of the caring landlord, to which the extensive improvements on his Estate bear eloquent witness, and of a sympathetic employer who provided pensions for long-serving employees and, against the advice of his Steward, reduced their working hours. As his Steward Lipscombe testified, "the welfare and comfort of the working classes on his property have been Mr Rolle's peculiar care". He was a man of simple religious faith and innate kindliness.

He was also conscientious in dealing, thoughtfully and promptly, with the numerous matters brought to his attention by his Stewards, or as we would say land agents. As far as the South Devon Estate was concerned, he may have been largely an absentee landlord but he was nevertheless in control of affairs, receiving thousands of letters from his Stewards over the years. He rarely wrote more than once a fortnight in reply, but his Stewards frequently attended upon him to receive instructions, even on comparatively minor matters. It would have been an unwise Steward who took too much upon himself in matters of expenditure and policy decisions.

In the context of this book, Mark Rolle's most significant action was the appointment in 1865, the year of the Rolle Estate Act, of Richard Hartley Lipscomb as Steward of the South Devon Estate. As we shall see in the next chapter, he was the most influential of the Stewards who served Mark Rolle in that capacity.

Syon House, East Budleigh: home of the Stewards.

Tidwell Barton Cottages, East Budleigh 1868.

THE STEWARDS

Three Stewards, or land agents, served the Estate during Mark Rolle's time. Samuel Taylor Coldridge was Steward from 1840 to 1865, Robert Hartley Lipscomb from 1865 to 1892 and Edwin Francis Chamier from 1892 to 1915. Before considering them individually, it is worth looking at what makes a good land agent. "The Book of the Landed Estate" published in 1869 by Robert Brown gives a contemporary view.

After some side-swipes at the inadequacy as land agents, of lawyers, members of the landlord's family, men of practical experience only, and, worst of all, youngsters with no more than a theoretical education, he concludes that what is required is a blend of practical experience and theoretical study, based on a good general education. He also favours a country upbringing.

The ideal training would begin with one year "with a high-class farmer – not as an onlooker, but as a workman, and on the distinct understanding that he is to have a hand in all the different branches of work". This would be followed by another similar year, but in a different county to broaden his experience, before going on to an Agricultural College where the young man should acquire a knowledge of "the sciences bearing on agriculture."

"As the next step, he should endeavour to get employed in the office of a good land surveyor for at least one year" to gain experience of measuring and valuing land. "He should afterwards engage himself as an assistant in the office of some land agent . . . on an estate where extensive improvements are being carried out."

After all this, which would have taken at least five years, Brown observes that there are still some men who, despite being well-trained, are "not qualified to conduct all the business devolving on an estate agent in a satisfactory manner". An aspiring land agent also needs "a cool and calculating turn of mind", and, in order to be fair to both landlord and tenant, "a clear judgement in regard to everything he engages in." Last but not least, he needs "a considerable amount of patience and frankness, combined with acuteness."

What a paragon the land agent should be, and how high his purpose! "The agent, when thoroughly qualified, ought to be, and really is, the great promoter of agricultural improvement on the estate . . . Nor is the influence of a man of that description confined to those in whom he is more immediately interested, for it is felt outside that circle . . . effecting an amount of good which it is impossible to estimate."

The remainder of Brown's book sets out, in an aggressively self-confident manner, the working knowledge which the well-equipped land agent should have. In addition to farming practices, this includes a fair knowledge of law (particularly in relation to tenancies), land improvement techniques including drainage and the use of manures, steam power, portable railways, fences and walls, road-making and embankments, farm buildings and cottages, game, forestry, water supply, valuation of land, and rent collection – in all nearly five hundred pages of solid, detailed information.

Samuel Taylor Coldridge (1799-1871)

Not every land agent (indeed perhaps few) had all the training, experience and knowledge that Brown advocated. Coldridge, Mark Rolle's first Steward, for example, appears to have had no previous experience of estate management. His father was a mapmaker and land surveyor working in Exeter. When Samuel grew up, he joined his father in his work. Together they did valuations for the Diocese of Exeter, and they were for a time surveyors to the Exeter Commissioners of Improvements. By 1834, however, major schemes were being proposed by the Commissioners, including the viaduct in North Street. The Coldridges considered that their salary was only commensurate with "their daily and ordinary business", and not with schemes of such magnitude, which were in any case beyond their competence. So they resigned. Judging by their letter of resignation, they did so with some relief at being free of "the agitated state of your Committee and General meetings." Work for the Exeter Diocese continued for only another five years. With work declining and the premature loss of his wife, Samuel must have been more than ready to build his life elsewhere. The opportunity, a golden one, came in 1840 when he was appointed as Steward to the South Devon Rolle Estate at the age of 40. He moved first to East Budleigh with his brother and sister, and later to Syon House, now the Estate Office, where his widowed mother also joined the family party. Syon House may well have been built for the purpose. Previously, the Stewards lived at Tidwell House.

For 25 years, he served as Steward. Towards the end of his term, he set in motion what was to become a major reorganization of the Estate under the energetic direction of his successor. He retired at the age of 65 and went to live in Exmouth, where he died of apoplexy six years later.

Despite his previous lack of experience as a land agent, the fact that he held the post of Steward for so many years says something about his character and ability, although his successor Lipscomb had no high opinion of him. He refers to "the imbecility of my worthy but worn-out predecessor", presumably referring to Coldridge's declining years. It is intriguing to speculate about his departure in 1865, the year of the Rolle Estate Act. Did the Trustees suggest that he should make way for a younger man, one moreover of wider experience, to oversee the programme of improvements on the Estate?

Robert Hartley Lipscomb (1834 – 1892)

Lipscomb, a North Country man, was much closer to Robert Brown's ideal. When Mark Rolle appointed him as Steward in 1865, he was 31 years of age but already an experienced land agent. It is obvious from the style of his letters that he had been well educated. The details of his professional training are unclear, but he was certainly country-bred. His father was Rector of Welbury near Northallerton in Yorkshire.

In articles written in later life entitled "Old Hints to Young Land Agents", he says, "I suppose that even when quite a lad I knew I was interested in numbers of the rents paid in that district and their rates per acre. I then spent several years in the county which I should recommend almost before any other county as a tuition ground for agency . . . in Northumberland, and there I had, and took, abundant chances of learning the value of properties and of individual fields." In one of his letters, he refers to being with Sir Walter Trevelyan's Agent in Northumberland.

He goes on, "From thence I got my first agency in a stonewall county." This was probably Yorkshire since, in another letter about a possible reading room and library in Otterton, he writes, "In a village in Yorkshire, I nearly ruined the Public House by establishing a cheerful well-lighted room which was open nightly from 7 till 9.30." Elsewhere, he refers to four years spent in Scotland as Factor of an estate in Ross-shire, so he had much and varied experience before he came to Devon.

He is silent on whether he had attended Agricultural College, as recommended by Brown. However, few land agents at that time would have had this opportunity as the only one, the Royal College at Cirencester, did not open until 1845 although Edinburgh University ran a course in Agriculture. He writes of his "tutor", probably an established land agent to whom he was an assistant. He himself had pupils in his time. In any event, he would have studied books on land agency, as Brown's treatise was by no means the first on the subject. The Estate Archives contain a copy of "British Farming" by John Wilson published in 1862. At about this time, the same publishers issued "Elements of Agricultural Chemistry".

As Steward, Lipscomb lived at Syon House with his wife and children, and three servants. On a salary of £500 a year, he was comfortably off, and he and his wife were both prominent in the local community. He served as Churchwarden at All Saints, East Budleigh and was active in the management of the local schools.

Apparently he started as Steward for the South Devon Estate only, but in 1875 took charge of the North Devon Estate as well. Although he made lengthy visits in the north, he must have had a permanent deputy there.

He held the post of Steward for the Estate for 27 years before retiring because of ill health at a comparatively early age. During those 27 years, he oversaw momentous changes on the Estate as farm sizes were increased by amalgamation, and new farms and cottages were built.

Higher Knowle Farm, Budleigh Salterton 1869.

He was eager to raise the standard of farming on the Estate. He floated a scheme to send tenants to study the superior methods practised in Northumberland and Lothian. He persuaded Mark Rolle to offer a cup to be presented annually to the tenant with the tidiest farm of more than 100 (later 50) acres.

He became sufficiently well known and respected in his profession to be called in 1881 to give evidence, as one of the few witnesses from the south-west, before the Royal Commission on Agricultural Depression chaired by the Duke of Richmond.

He was also asked to contribute a series of articles to the monthly "Land Agents Record" in 1889 and 1890. These articles were entitled "Old Hints to Young Land Agents", and are a delight to read. Lively, witty and shrewd, they give a flavour of the man's character, which can also perhaps be read from his portrait, and is certainly confirmed by his letter books.

"Old Hints" give a fascinating insight into his methods, and some idea of the great scope of the responsibilities of an agent, who, provided he stood well with his principal, had immense authority on his estate. It is impossible to pass by these articles without indulging in a few quotations, from which we can learn something of the nature of his work in his own words.

On Relations with his Principal: "Let me impress upon the young agent with my utmost earnestness to be perfectly frank and above board with his chief. If he has the ill-luck to make some miscalculation or mistake, and has either wasted some money in some unsuccessful venture or experiment, or, what is more likely, has allowed some specious rascal to get on his blind side, let him be the first to let his chief hear about it, and all about it. Never, under any circumstances, leave anything to be found out against you; never understate any loss, failure, or bad business of any sort. If you don't entirely trust your chief, how can you expect him entirely to trust you?

On the Use of Estate Staff: "Young Agent may take my word for it that, if success attends his efforts, he can no more depute the real brain work of his business to underlings than a successful painter or lawyer can do so. Book-keepers, surveyors, plan drawers, shorthand writers, clerks of works, foresters, bailiffs can all be got by the score at £100 a year salaries, but they are all tools in the agent's hands. If they are tools that think for him, as well as carrying out his instructions, they are of double use to him and are worth double pay, and are cheap at the price."

On the Right Use of Time: "Remember that an agent's life above all others, a parson's included, may be a very busy one, or the reverse, just as he himself makes it. Nothing is easier than to throw plenty of cold water on proposals which would benefit your charge and enhance its value, but which would give you a lot of personal trouble. Nothing is easier than to let things slide."

On Farm Tenants: "Young Agent must take care to make himself accessible to farmers and to business callers generally. On at least one day in each week, he ought to be "at home". What can be more trying than for a man to ride or travel many miles for an interview only to be disappointed ?" and "If any request is simply ungrantable, tell your man so plainly. Never let a man go away with the hope that you are going to say "Yes" when you are inwardly resolving to write him a decided "No", for that is simply moral cowardice."

On Repairs: "In Utopia, if estates do not manage themselves, agents will, I take it, be relieved from all anxiety on the subject of repairs; for if there is one enemy who can never be subdued in this work-a-day world on which we agents exercise our calling, it is the enemy of decay." And "If the young land agent escapes with one letter or call per month from tenants of gentlemen's houses let under yearly tenancies, he may think himself lucky . . . Don't I see in my mind's eye, when I show myself on any public occasion, my gentleman tenant spot me, edge round me, descend upon me with affected surprise, and remark on the weather, and then, after a very short pause, comes the "Oh, Mr Victim, it seems a shame to bother you with business here, but (the inevitable but) I do wish you would come and see how my dining-room chimney smokes" or "how my drawing-room wall is showing damp" or "what a suspicious smell there is, etc, etc." He always wants you to go and see his particular want personally, too, and why I never can tell, unless he thinks that you, as "boss", can lay your hand upon the place and cure it then and there. On the other hand, the patience of the cottager class under neglect, inconvenience, and even danger, is often beyond belief. "Us aren't been able to apse up the front door night-times, more than a year, but us don't take no notice o' un. Who'd a think of robbing the likes o' we?""

On Valuing Property: "I know that some people imagine that you might take a valuer 100 miles blindfold, drag him out of a train at a country railway station, and that he would be quite able to start off in any direction and value a farm, field by field, and, at the end of his inspection, name a fair rent then and there. My impression is that Mr Valuer, however experienced, would under those circumstances act very much as a liberated pigeon would under similar circumstances, and take his bearings very carefully indeed, and do a great deal of "circling" before taking any decided action. Some people imagine that valuers carry spades with them, and dig into the soil in order to see what it is like! Such a thing might be resorted to if the ground was covered in snow. I never saw a valuer do such a thing, and in my opinion, a valuer must be a poor one indeed if the eye of experience could not see much deeper than he could dig."

On the Profession: "Do what you can to elevate your profession. It is an honourable one. There is nothing in the work which is expected of us which need in any way be galling or lowering to a man of honour . . . Our power for good or evil in this world's affairs in a countryside is enormous. You may do much, very much, to make many hundreds of people of all grades prosperous and contented, or the reverse . . . I thank God that I am what I am. And if you are a lover of nature as well as of your work; if every bird and beast of the field, every flower of the hedgerow, every change of the developing season, every geological change on your charge, and all that such change brings with it, have an interest for you, and if your barometer, thermometer and rain-gauge have the same; if you are blessed (great blessing) with a cheery manner and a faculty for setting people at their ease and drawing them out; if you can throw off the vexations of your life as a duck does the water from its back, and if you have a receptiveness for all that is original and humorous, how can your life ever be dull? How can it be otherwise than full of interest, and therefore of happiness? But far and away above any satisfaction of this kind . . . is the inward knowledge that you can look the whole world in the face and say that you have done your duty, and something more than your duty."

There writes a man supremely happy in his work, and his letters tell the same story. From these articles, and even more from his letter books, we get to know the man well. In his neat handwriting, he filled 29½ letter

E. Budleigh. January 21. 1871 - Saty Night

Dear Sir,

I have today closed my 1870 accounts & have got out all the payments & receipts under the proper heads & detailed them on the enclosed abstract which I hope you will be able to devote a little time to, because I am, and always have been, anxious to put my employer in possession of each years transaction as early as possible in order that he may make any suggestions of reform before the new year has been far entered upon – An abstract must of necessity be meagre in information but I shall be only too glad to send you the details of any Branch of Receipts or payments on which you may wish for full information – I will add some remarks –

1 <u>Receipts.</u>

1. The balance _____ the year was quite £1000 to _____ Tax being payable in Jan _____ his having quite unexpectedly to _____ me I was obliged to draw _____ ount with Messrs Sanders _____ ldings as early as Febru _____ Deer 1870 a, you will see, a _____ January.

3 <u>Rock Ren</u> _____ any half years in hand _____ of the untoward season been b _____ e of, but there has still been a considerable increase in the Receipts as compared with 1869, and every man in arrears has been

R. H. Lipscomb, Steward, and a sample of his letters.

books with copies of his letters. All but one of these are in the Rolle Estate Archives; unfortunately the first book is missing. Each volume contains about 1,600 letters, close to 50,000 letters in all.

The letters range widely over all manner of subjects - letters on expenditure, on the repair of properties, on building new farm buildings and cottages, letters to Mr Forster (Mark Rolle's solicitor in London) for advice on legal matters, letters on tenancies and rents, on valuations, on letting land for building in Budleigh Salterton and Exmouth, letters on bricks and timber, letters to the forester and the bailiff of the Home Farm. Last but not least, there are highly diplomatic (but never obsequious) letters to the formidable Lady Louisa Rolle written in the third person. "Mr Lipscomb presents his compliments to Lady Rolle and begs to say . . ."

In his industrious way, with good sense and touches of humour, he dealt with all manner of subjects, both great and small. Not the least of his concerns was the rabbit population. At one point, he became so exasperated with the farmers' frequent complaints about the damage they caused that he burst out "I am sure that for my part I have every wish never to hear the subject of Rabbits mentioned again."

He was to be disappointed. The rabbit problem was a very serious one. The Estate paid out hundreds of pounds to tenant farmers in compensation for damage caused by rabbits. The root of the problem was Lady Rolle, who apparently had a right to all the rabbits on the Estate. Her warreners however took no more than 20 or 30 rabbits a night which did little to control, let alone reduce, the rabbit population. There was widespread resentment among the tenants, made more bitter by the knowledge that Lady Rolle was actually selling the rabbits that fed so freely on their crops.

Eventually, Mark Rolle authorized his tenants to kill rabbits on their land. Lady Rolle was greatly displeased, and blamed Lipscomb. He defended himself by claiming that he had acted "in exact accordance with Mr Rolle's instructions". This was a trifle disingenuous of him since for some time he had been urging Mark Rolle to this course. But then Lipscomb, whom some accused of being a Radical, was far from popular with Lady Rolle, complaining "the manner in which Lady Rolle writes and speaks of me is what I scarcely know how to endure silently". No wonder he ceased to have any direct communication with her, preferring to use

Forster, the solicitor, as a go-between.

And all through the books, there are of course letters to his "chief", reporting, seeking instructions, and even soliciting help for others. "Something turns up every day now for me to trouble you about. I am asked to entreat you to give an increased subscription to Exmouth regatta and athletic sports."

It is a great pity that his Stewardship came to a sad and untimely conclusion when he was only 58. Near the end, his son Basil, already assistant Steward, took over much of his father's work. In a letter of January 1892, he writes "The Doctors have ordered my Father, who has this week had a relapse, to give up all work and worry of every sort for at least three months. I therefore acknowledge your letter of yesterday's date . . .and have not shown it to my Father as we have to keep all letters from him."

Despite this, Lipscomb evidently rallied, for in March he wrote a long letter to Mark Rolle in which he urged his chief to carry on the "good work" of improving the farms and cottages on the Estate "until the work is completed".

At about this time, he took himself off to Madeira in hope of recovery from what he described as "congestion of the liver with complications". He sent optimistic reports to his family but he died there on 18 May. The obituary in the East Budleigh Parish Magazine is such a moving tribute to the man that it is worth quoting in full.

"One of the widest known and most esteemed of our parishioners has, in the Providence of God, been called away to a better world. The familiar face, the animated manner, the eager spirit of ROBERT HARTLEY LIPSCOMB will long be remembered by old friends here, and in almost every home standing on the extensive Rolle Estates, both in North and South Devon. Those who knew him best knew well what a gentle sympathetic heart he possessed, and all can testify to his unswerving devotion to duty, his indefatigable industry and his loyalty to those whom for 27 years he here so faithfully served. But incessant work, and the countless responsibilities incident to his position told on a constitution not naturally strong, and after six month's illness, borne with Christian bravery and patience, in which he never altogether lost his winning cheerfulness and brightness, he peacefully entered on his rest on Wednesday, May 18th, in the 59th year of his age. He will be sorely missed and his memory will long be cherished with affection by the large circle of friends and acquaintances, which seemed to widen indefinitely with increasing years. He will be remembered as a faithful steward of upright purpose and integrity, a generous and kind friend to all, a man of the widest sympathies, a charming companion, a devout Christian, and a loyal Churchman. The writer might say much more out of a full heart, but will add only this of him; that the better he was known, the more he was loved."

To sum up his Stewardship of the Estate, one can do no better than to quote Mark Rolle's tribute to him. "His services on behalf of my property I can never sufficiently acknowledge."

His son Basil continued to act as Steward for some months. However, there is a certain tentativeness about his letters, which suggests that he was not quite up to the job. He was, after all, only 23 years old. He stayed on for a time as assistant to the new Steward.

Edwin Francis Chamier (1848 – 1916)

Chamier came from a very different background to Lipscomb. He was educated at Winchester and Oxford, and was subsequently called to the Bar. Like many lawyers in earlier centuries, he then transferred his attention to the management of landed estates. He acted as agent for the Rev. Lord J Thynne and Lord Stanhope, at Stratton, Cornwall from 1878 to 1892, before his appointment as Steward of the Rolle Estate.

Inevitably he lacked Lipscomb's intimate knowledge of farming and, although he too was a prolific letter writer (filling 25 letter books), his letters make dull reading compared to those of his predecessor. They are strictly, often tersely, confined to the matters in hand, and reveal little of the writer's personality. One senses that he did not have the self-confidence of Lipscomb, nor perhaps his enjoyment of life, although Chamier's obituary does refer to his "genial disposition".

Any steward of a major landowner such as Mark Rolle could hardly fail to be well known in his profession. It is no surprise therefore to find that Chamier was a member of the committee of the Society of Landed Estate Agents when it was formed in 1901.

Chamier took over the management of the Estate at a difficult time. The depression in agriculture was deepening. In January 1893 he had to write sixteen letters pressing major tenants for serious arrears of rent. To make matters worse, he was required to subsidise the North Devon Estate from that in the south (which was now referred to as the East Devon Estate). When presenting the accounts for the year ending 31 December 1892, he observed, "The resources of this property have been strained to their utmost to afford relief to the North Devon Estate". He also complained of "a depression on prices of stock, and difficulty of sale".

Moreover the Estate no longer had the services of Robert Kingdom, the experienced and hard-working clerk of works. Chamier brought in a man from the North Devon Estate although Mark Rolle had expressed reservations about his strength of character. However Chamier considered that he could himself make good this deficiency.

Later in his stewardship he had to adjust to a change of Chief when Mark Rolle died in 1907, and was succeeded by the 21st Lord Clinton.

By December 1914, his health had by his own account "broken down altogether". He wrote, "The doctor will not hear of my going on beyond such time as will enable Lord Clinton to find a successor". He stayed on until the middle of January 1915, before retiring to Bude where he died in November 1916, aged 68.

Perhaps it says something about the onerous nature of the job that these last two Stewards both had to give up because of serious ill health.

E. F. Chamier, Steward.
From the Devon & Exeter Gazette.

Seaview Farm, Ladram Road, Otterton 1865.

Weeks Farm, Pinn Lane, Otterton 1869.

THE ECONOMIC AND SOCIAL BACKGROUND AND "HIGH FARMING"

While it is not essential for the purpose of this book to delve deeply into the history of agriculture, some understanding of the subject does help to place the building programme on the Rolle Estate in the latter half of the 19th century in its historical context.

The wholesale enclosure of open land in the 18th century created great unified estates where, under the control of the landowner and his agent, the land was cultivated by leasehold tenant farmers employing landless labourers.

It was on these broad acres that the Agricultural Revolution erupted. The enclosures prepared the ground upon which the new, more scientific approach to agriculture could flourish. Nor was this concept attractive to the landowner alone. Many tenant farmers also embraced its tenets willingly, while others were induced to do so by the terms of their leases.

A scientific system of crop rotation evolved, pioneered by such men as "Turnip" Marquis Townshend, Coke of Norfolk and Arthur Young, the chief advocate of enclosure. New methods of drainage, drilling, sowing and manuring resulted in increased yields from the farm lands. The introduction of root crops not only kept the land in good heart but also provided winter feed for cattle and sheep. Wholesale slaughter of stock in the autumn was rendered unnecessary, a clear inducement to improve the quality of the animals themselves. Owners took pride in the improvements in their flocks, hence the spate of static portraits showing a corpulent farm animal, with the robust owner or breeder at its head. Often it is hard to tell which looks more smug, the man or the beast.

The Napoleonic Wars brought benefits to the agricultural economy. The inevitable restriction on imports led to an increased demand for homegrown produce. Cobbett on his travels in 1821 was met with the toast "Here's to another war or a bad harvest!" The desire for a "bad harvest" can be linked to grain prices. In a year of glut, demand did not increase by much, even though prices were very low, for there was a limit to the demand. But when a bad harvest led to a meagre production of grain, this demand created disproportionately high prices.

It also happened that the period of the Wars coincided with a succession of poor harvests, so the farmers enjoyed a double benefit in accordance with their toast. At the outbreak of war in 1793, the price of wheat stood at 44 shillings per quarter. Towards the end of the war, the average was around 102 shillings. While farmers and landowners profited, that was no consolation to the poor, who faced near famine conditions.

After 1815, when the profitable wartime abnormalities gradually came to an end, the good times for farming were over, at least for the time being. And the recklessness with which landowners had over-invested in schemes of improvement, raising huge loans to do so, often at steep rates of interest, came home to roost.

Fear of economic failure began to haunt the farming community as the restraints on imports were now removed. The farmers' reaction was to put pressure on the government to protect their interests. Nor was the government able to ignore their pleas, as agriculture contributed over a third of the national income, gave employment to the same proportion of the employed population, and provided all but a tiny proportion of the nation's food.

So, in 1815, a new Corn Law was passed to give some protection against foreign imports of grain. This measure engendered a fierce debate between protectionists and anti-protectionists, which lasted until the Repeal of the Corn Laws in 1846. Despite the new Corn Law, and subsequent modifications regulating the import of grain, the farming industry continued to decline. Grain prices slipped steadily from 75 shillings a quarter in 1815 to 53 shillings in 1846. Moreover, during the post-war depression, bad harvests often reduced the British farmers' share of the home market, the balance being met by imported grain. A bad harvest was no longer the boon it had been. To make matters worse a series of outbreaks of disease ravaged flocks and herds.

William Cobbett wrote in his "Rural Rides" in 1821 "nothing can be clearer than that the present race of farmers, generally speaking, must be swept away by bankruptcy if they do not, in time, make their bow and retire."

In 1846, the great controversy over the Corn Laws came to a dramatic conclusion. The Corn Laws were repealed. The Anti Corn Law League and its allies had triumphed. They argued successfully that a free market for food would put more money into people's pockets to spend on consumer goods, and also encourage reciprocal trade with the principal food-exporting countries. The farming community of course viewed it differently, fearing the competition from abroad. At first these fears seemed to be realized, as the price of grain continued to fall significantly from 1846 to 1852. However there followed a quarter of a century of comparative stability and prosperity that was later invested with nostalgia as "the Golden Age".

Part of the reason why agriculture weathered the repeal of the Corn Laws during this period was a rapid increase in population, which created a larger home market for farm produce. Between 1801 and 1851, the population of England and Wales rose from 9 million to 18 million. Also, foreign competition remained for a time comparatively insignificant, and the development of railways cut the farmers' transport costs.

At the same time, the great scientific and technological advances of the 19th century were beginning to be applied to agriculture, making it more efficient and productive. This was a key element in the spread of "High Farming" as it came to be known.

The most influential advocate of "High Farming" at this time was Sir James Caird. He came to prominence in 1848 with the publication of his pamphlet "High Farming, the Best Solution for Protection". He pressed for large farms where a high level of investment would be worthwhile, and where full advantage could be taken of the new scientific knowledge of soils and how to treat them. This included drainage, the use of chemical fertilisers and the growth of special crops. New buildings, new roads and new machinery were also essential in his view, as well as the use of the railway to take goods to market.

The most important improvement of all at this time was in drainage, especially on heavy clay soils. The system of digging trenches across fields was inconvenient and expensive. However, the problem was overcome by the introduction in the 1840's of the tile drain, and the invention of machinery like the mole drainage plough for laying the tiles with the minimum of disturbance and at greatly reduced cost.

A better understanding of the chemical aspects of agriculture led to the use of fertilisers to augment animal manure and bone meal, both of which were inevitably limited resources. Superphosphate and basic slag were available in Britain as products of the Industrial Revolution, but guano (bird manure) had to be imported from Peru, while nitrate came from Chile and, from the 1860s, potash from Germany. Imports of these fertilisers soared.

During the 1840s and 1850s, the agricultural engineering industry blossomed. A host of new machines came onto the market – ploughs, harrows, tedders (for tossing hay), drills, cultivators, reapers and threshing machines. With the introduction of steam power, the farming scene was transformed, as steam threshing became increasingly widespread.

The pace at which these changing methods were adopted had much to do with the written word. Caird followed his earlier pamphlet with a major book, "English Agriculture in 1850-51". From 1840 on, the Royal Agricultural Society, presided over by the progressive and scientifically inclined Philip Pusey, himself a farming squire, published articles covering a wide range of investigations into the effectiveness of manures, the feeding of livestock, and crop diseases.

Ambitious and determined promoters of agricultural improvements built model experimental farms. And, to complete the picture, the first agricultural college was founded at Cirencester in 1845 with the express aim of teaching the sons of tenant farmers "the science of Agriculture and the various sciences connected therewith, and the practical application thereof to the cultivation of the soil, and the rearing and management of stock".

Agriculture had come a very long way in less than a hundred years, from a craft to a science, but over-enthusiasm brought dangers of its own.

The innovations in buildings and machinery were very costly. Caird was practical enough to realize that investment must be undertaken with an eye to higher profits (hence his recommendation that the ideal farm should consist of at least 300 acres, whereas the average farm in 1851 was little more than 100 acres). Unfortunately, however, it became a point of honour with some landowners to embrace every possible improvement, regardless of whether it actually increased profits. The Duke of Northumberland, for instance, invested nearly £1,000,000 on his estate for a trifling 2½% return, which he could have got from Government stocks without any effort. Little of the capital invested in this way could ever be recouped.

In the depression which followed "the Golden Age", the great landed aristocracy were to regret this reckless laying-out of capital, which contributed to their own decline in the later years of the 19th century.

Even those landowners like Mark Rolle who could hardly be called reckless, yet who started late upon the business of improvement, were to lose heavily when agriculture declined.

Of course it has to be recognized that, alongside "High Farming" on the large estates, what I suppose should be called "Low Farming" continued on the small independent farms. Of those who farmed more than 5 acres, about 60% occupied less than 100 acres. Unless they were under the direction of a landowner who stipulated how they were to farm, they would have been disinclined, or indeed unable, to go in for much "High Farming". In this respect, the Rolle Estate, despite attempts to increase the size of its numerous small farms, was also at a disadvantage when it came to applying the principles of "High Farming". It was not unusual in being composed of small farms. Farms of 300 acres or more were still comparatively rare. Clapham in his "Economic History of Modern Britain" computed that, in 1851, of the 215,571 farms in the country, only 16,671 were of that size, whereas there were 134,700 of less than 100 acres.

In the mid 1870s, a chill wind began to blow on the farming scene. The protectionists who had fought hard to retain the Corn Laws found belated justification as imports of cheap grain flowed more and more abundantly from the cornfields of America, Canada, the Baltic lands and Russia. Meanwhile, at home, British farmers, and particularly those in the southwest, had to contend with an extraordinary succession of extreme weather conditions for 20 years after 1874. Writing in 1882, Lipscomb reckoned that " seven tenths of all the troubles that have come upon farmers are the result of bad seasons".

The price of wheat dropped from 55 shillings a quarter in 1870 to about 30 shillings in the early 1890s, when wheat imports represented over three quarters of the nation's consumption. The repeal of the Corn Laws was a victory for the town over the countryside. Cheap bread for urban dwellers meant poor prices for farmers.

To make matters worse for the farming community, by 1880, refrigerated meat began to arrive in ever increasing quantities from New Zealand and Australia. In 1895, 28% of the beef and veal, 31% of the mutton and lamb, and 49% of the pig meat consumed in Britain came in from abroad. Meat prices fell by about 25% between 1883 and 1887, and continued to fall, although at a slower rate.

Kingston Farm, Stowford Hill, Colaton Raleigh 1873.

Wynhay House, East Budleigh 1879.

Two factors prevented the import of foodstuffs from becoming a total disaster for farming. Production costs, apart from labour, were falling, and the population rose dramatically so the market was continually expanding.

In response to these changing hostile conditions, those farmers who could turned from the classic mixed arable system, where crops and animals supported each other, to concentrate on those areas where markets were more favourable – livestock, dairying, vegetables or fruit. Lipscomb did all he could to encourage this changeover on the Estate. But the conversion required capital, which was in short supply. The big landowners, who had already over-committed themselves financially, now had to accept a lower income from their land as falling prices forced down rents from tenant farmers.

By the end of the century, agriculture was no longer the nation's major industry. The steep decline in profitability, allied to the Government's taxation policies, led to the break up of the great estates, and with it the pattern of rural life as it had existed for centuries.

In the context of this book, it is interesting to note that Mark Rolle's building programme on the Rolle Estate ran on well beyond the so-called "Golden Age" (which was over by 1875) into the times of depression. As agricultural prices fell, tenant farmers experienced greater and greater difficulty in finding the rent on quarter day. The relations between landlord and tenant were inevitably put under strain, and even, in time, those between landlord and steward.

A quotation from James Loch, most famous of all the 19th century land agents, sets the scene for the next chapter. "The property of a great English Nobleman must be managed on the same principle as a little kingdom, not like the affair of a little merchant. The future and lasting interest and honour of the family as well as their immediate income must be kept in view, while a merchant thinks only of his daily profits and his own immediate life interests".

Houghton Farm, Ottery Road: Granary 1876

THE BUILDING PROGRAMME

It is possible that a few of the farm buildings on the Estate were built in the time of John, Lord Rolle, or during the minority of Mark Rolle. However, the major programme of improvements did not get under way until the 1860s. It may be said to start from Coldridge's report in 1861.

This report listed the properties on the Estate parish by parish, noting the condition of each one. Of the properties in Otterton and East Budleigh, about a third are described, in whole or in part, as "bad" or "very bad". Others are described as "very old", which might imply that their condition was poor.

As a probable consequence of this survey, an advertisement was placed in Trewman's Exeter Flying Post in April 1864, inviting builders to tender for the erection of four sets of new farm buildings and four new farmhouses. The farms referred to included Hayes Farm, East Budleigh, and Pinn and Northmostown farms in Otterton. Hayes Farm was presumably at Hayes Barton, but whether the proposed work was in respect of the farm complex by the road, or the farm buildings attached to the old Barton is not clear.

The Pinn referred to is almost certainly what is now known as Lower Pinn Farm. Although Cherry and Peysner in "The Buildings of England; Devon" state that the farm buildings were erected in 1851 "one of the earliest examples of the Rolle rebuilding programme", the farmhouse, with its traditional Georgian sash windows was built in 1864 to the design of the architect Joseph Rowell of Newton Abbot. (The date of 1881 on the small gable at the west end is misleading and must refer to a later addition). Northmostown Farm was the result of an amalgamation of a number of smaller holdings consolidated to form a viable farm unit.

What is interesting about this advertisement of 1864 is the use of outside agents. The plans and specifications were to be inspected at the office of Messrs Drew and Sons, surveyors in Exeter. Further information could be obtained from the architect, Joseph Rowell or from John Drew, to whom the tenders were to be returned.

The use of outside agencies did not appeal to Lipscomb. From the time

Dalditch Farm, Dalditch Lane, East Budleigh 1879.

Rolle Barton, Otterton 1867.

he was appointed Steward in 1865, significantly the same year as the passing of the Rolle Estate Act, the scope and pace of the programme of improvements intensified. A more positive direction is discernible.

After making his own appraisal of the conditions on the whole Estate, and preparing a comprehensive plan of repairs and improvements, he took matters very much into his own hands. When tenders were invited again in the Exeter Flying Post in August 1867 for buildings in Littleham, the advertisement stated, "Plans and specifications from Mr Lipscomb, East Budleigh". Furthermore, tenders were to be returned to him. He was by now firmly in charge.

In a letter to Mark Rolle in December 1867, he made his position quite clear. "Many Agents decline altogether to take the responsibility and call in professional Architects and Clerks of Works for the building… Other Agents take the trouble irresponsibly and charge a percentage upon their account expected for themselves. I neither wish to call in any professional men, nor do I wish to charge, nor have I ever charged, any percentage".

There was a great deal needing to be done. In March 1867 Lipscomb wrote to Mark Rolle, "There is no question which gives me so much anxiety as the buildings. I have daily complaints from the tenants of the state of their buildings, and endless demands, which I cannot call unjust, for expenditure… The number of buildings upon the Property is so enormous that there is a very great deal to be done, and in common fairness to many of the tenants who have literally no decent buildings, I do not see my way to an immediate reduction in expenditure".

Looking back in 1883, Lipscomb commented, "Mr Rolle inherited a Property which had scarcely one complete set of Farm Buildings upon it, and in my first few rounds upon the Property in November 1865, I saw 18 sets of Farm Buildings entirely consisting of cob and thatch which had either actually fallen, or which had been cobbled until they would cobble no longer".

The late 1860s, 1870s and 1880s were therefore a period of intense building activity on the Estate. When Lipscomb retired in 1892, most, if not all of the farms had been improved by new buildings, and very many new cottages had been built. The farm buildings and cottages so far identified are listed in Appendix A.

Stowford Farmhouse, Colaton Raleigh 1884.

Passaford Farm, Ottery Road, Otterton 1886.

What was going forward on the Rolle Estate was little different to what was happening elsewhere on progressive estates where High Farming was in favour. The first impulse was to improve, and in many cases to rebuild, farm buildings. It is not too much of an exaggeration to say that these were now regarded as components of an agricultural factory. The example of burgeoning manufacturing industries spread to agriculture. Many who had made fortunes in industrial enterprises invested in land, creating their own landed estates. The second impulse was to improve the quality of farmhouses in order to attract and retain the best tenant farmers.

The last impulse was to improve the quality of labourers' cottages. The motive for this was in part philanthropic, drawing its strength from Victorian piety and a growing concern for the health and sanitation of rural communities, but it was also allied to a more cynical consideration. As one writer put it, the labouring classes were "living engines" which needed to be looked after in order to function efficiently for their employers, a view which Mark Rolle would surely have found highly distasteful.

Farm and Cottage Tenancies
Before looking at the building works, we should take account of the Leases on the Estate. They are an important factor in our story. In the earlier years at least, they dictated the pace of change, and in later years determined how the land was to be farmed.

The tenanted properties, whether farm or cottage, were customarily held on Reversionary Leases, or Leases for Life, so-called because the term for this type of lease was 99 years or up to Three Lives. This requires a word of explanation. Broadly speaking, on the tenant's side, up to three persons would be named. The first would be the original lessee; on his death, the lease would revert to the second named person and, when he died, to the third.

As the third named person was often a very young child, the terms of the lease on any reasonable calculation could be a very long one, even if it was unlikely to run to 99 years. In any event it was from the outset, an indeterminate period. It might be many incalculable years before the property reverted to the landlord. The system was a serious handicap to any reorganization of the Estate.

Rolle Cottages, Knowle Village 1873.

On entering the tenancy, the tenant had to pay a fine, or fee, followed by an annual rent. This would amount to three or four pounds a year in the case of a cottage. A farmer would pay according to the rental value of his farm, perhaps between one and a half to two pounds an acre.

The lease required the tenant to keep the property in good repair, and the landlord could terminate the lease if this condition was not met. However none but the most hard-hearted landlord would readily evict a tenant on his Estate, even if the rent were in arrears. Indeed, in times of depression, it was difficult to find a good tenant for a tenantless farm.

It was largely to remedy the unsatisfactory situation caused by Reversionary Leases that the Rolle Estate Act was passed. One of its main provisions, which nevertheless took time to take effect throughout the Estate, empowered Mark Rolle to offer tenants an annuity for life in exchange for the remainder of their lease. Of course, he could not enforce acceptance, but it was unlikely that the tenant would refuse.

Early in his stewardship, Lipscomb prepared standard forms of leases for farms and cottages to replace the Reversionary Leases. In 1884, he prepared a new Farm Agreement which he discussed in draft form with the leading tenant farmers. After a few amendments at their request, it was finalized. The tenancy agreement for Watering Farm in Otterton is an example of its application.

There was much argument nationally at the time about the respective merits of yearly tenancies, and tenancies for a fixed period of years. One agent went so far as to declare "a tenancy from year to year is a complete ban to all improvements", arguing that such a tenancy would inhibit a good tenant from putting capital into the working of the farm. On the other hand, it was argued that a slip-shod farmer on a long lease could not be removed.

The new Farm Agreement seems to have taken account of both sides of the argument. Perhaps as a reaction to the severe handicaps associated with Reversionary Leases, it was for one year "and thenceforth from year to year until the Tenancy shall be determined". As determination was to be at 12 months' notice on either side, it was clearly the intention that the tenant should remain in possession so long as the rent was forthcoming (in the case of Watering Farm £59 per annum plus £19 for the Tithe) and so long as the tenant observed the other conditions of the lease.

Pitson Farm, Ottery Road, Newton Poppleford 1885.

Dotton Farm 1871.

Pitson Farm.

These conditions set out in some detail how the land was to be farmed. The tenant was to "manage and cultivate the lands according to the most approved course of husbandry" (that is, in accordance with the principles of High Farming). The terms of the lease covered manuring, crop rotation, yearly close cutting of hedges, and filling up orchards with new planting when necessary. The tenant was forbidden to break up any old pasture, to cut or prune any but fruit trees, or to destroy hedge banks. The preoccupations of the environmentalist are no new thing!

The tenant was to reside on the farm and keep it stocked (to the value of at least two years' rent). He was responsible for all internal repairs and redecoration of buildings. Draining and certain other improvements would be at the Landlord's expense, but for these he could charge the tenant 4% of the cost annually.

Although the Agreement expressly excluded the far-sighted provisions of the Agricultural Holdings Act of 1883, it nevertheless stated that compensation to the tenant for certain improvements should be paid by the landlord on determination of the tenancy as laid down by that Act. The other provisions of the Act were excluded not because they were more favourable to the tenants; they were less so. Indeed the Act had one unforeseen, but unfortunate, consequence for them. It proposed to limit the landlord's power of distraint. If a tenant were deeply in arrears, the landlord would only be empowered to distrain (that is, seize the tenant's possessions in lieu of rent owing) to an amount equivalent to one year's rental, thereby forfeiting any excess of arrears.

The plight of Charles Drake of Lower Pinn in 1880, which was not exceptional, shows how much Mark Rolle stood to lose when the Act took effect. The annual rent (including tithes) for the farm was £248. By Lady Day 1880, he owed £337, having paid no more than £70 in 1879, and only £89 in 1880. He was unlikely to do any better in 1881.

The only option left to Mark Rolle to counter the effects of the Act before it came into force was a harsh one – giving the tenant notice to quit on the grounds of breach of contract. It was a course he was reluctant to pursue, so we find Lipscomb urging defaulters to pay off a significant part of the arrears to avoid eviction. Not that this could save a Charles Drake. He could by no means pay more.

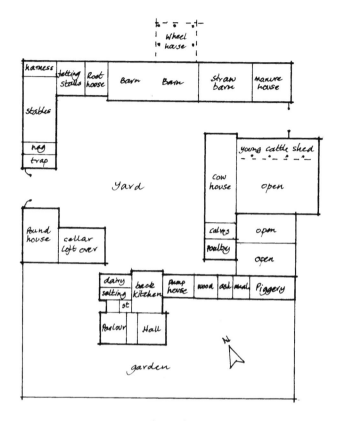

Fig 1: Diagrammatic Plan of Dotton Farm 1871.

Dotton Farm Barns 1871.

Farm Buildings

In parts of the country where farm sizes were large, the whole farm complex might be rebuilt entirely. Even in such cases, however, the capital outlay might not be commensurate with the increased rental value.

Given the smallness of the farms on the Rolle Estate in South Devon, and therefore the stark improbability of getting a satisfactory return on the capital outlay, the scale of the building programme was astonishing. Lipscomb, when submitting the 1870 accounts to Mark Rolle, admitted the outlay to "be out of all proportion to the rental".

The newly erected farm of 142½ acres at Seaview (originally Larderham) Farm illustrates the point. The farm cost £2,650 to build in 1867. It was let at an annual rent of £225 (plus £35 in lieu of tithes). That might have been a reasonable return on the capital expenditure if it had been possible to maintain the rental value in the times of depression. However, this was not to be the case. Lipscomb goes on to say that the expenditure on improvements could be reduced, but "that cannot be done without a very large decrease in the staff of workmen, and postponement for some years of very many needful cases of repair and renewal still existing". These economies were not implemented and the building programme went on apace.

The farms that were completely built from scratch included Lower Pinn, Seaview, Northmostown, and probably Higher Knowle, Houghton, and Hardys. Certainly Dotton was built as a replacement of a former farm sited on an unsuitable boggy location. The plans for the new farm at Dotton are still on display in the Estate office, signed by Robert Kingdom, Clerk of the Works.

From the diagrammatic plan in figure 1, it can be seen that the arrangement follows the standard contemporary pattern. The yard faces south to catch the sun, and is protected by the high barn to the north and the two storey building on the west side to give some shelter from the prevailing south-west winds. The stables face east to catch the rising sun for the benefit of the early rising carter and ploughman. They are also placed as far as possible from the piggeries, horses being thought peculiarly sensitive to unpleasant smells. The farmhouse is on the south side set back from the yard. Near it are the piggeries, which depended on the by-products of the dairy (on the north side of the house) and of the

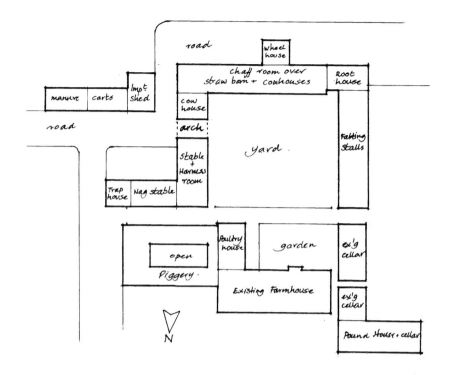

Fig 2: Diagrammatic Plan of South Farm, Otterton 1869.

South Farm: S E corner of yard.

household. Also close to the house is the poultry house, traditionally the concern of the farmer's wife. Completing the square is the lower range for cattle with their adjoining open yards, and the manure house conveniently at hand.

The buildings at South Farm, Otterton (figure 2) are also arranged around a square courtyard but here the orientation is completely different. This may have been governed by the presence of an existing farmhouse. It was also thought desirable that the highest range incorporating the barn should be on the seaward side to give shelter from winds blowing from that quarter.

There was hardly a farm on the estate which did not benefit to some extent from the programme of improvements. The Appendix lists those that have been identified. On some farms, all but the farmhouses were built at this time. This category includes South Farm, Hill Farm, Kingston, Passaford, Pavers, Drupe and Langsford.

A curious feature of the farms on the Estate, even that at Dotton, is the retention of the wheel house, where horse power was used to drive threshing machines etc., this at a time when steam power was being taken up enthusiastically elsewhere.

When new farm buildings were proposed at Tidwell in 1867 the tenant farmer asked for an Engine House, rather than a wheel shed, so that he could thresh by steam power. The additional expenditure was approved. According to a letter from Lipscomb, Mark Rolle "would like to see steam power at many of the Homesteads on the property". So it would appear that the reluctance to use steam power was due to the conservatism of the tenant farmers.

While the farm steadings were being improved, the existing farmhouses were normally retained. However, they were sometimes modernised, often by re-roofing. The old, possibly thatched, roof was replaced by a tiled or slated roof. Lipscomb had a prejudice against thatch. In the process the upper walls might be raised, and new windows inserted in the upper storey. Lemprice Farm is an example.

Flint Cottages, Yettington 1874.

Flint Cottages, Otterton 1875.

Cottages

The trend in land holding in the 18th and early 19th centuries was towards consolidation and expansion of landed estates, including the Rolle Estate. The great landlords swallowed up small estates and individual holdings. Farms grew in size and, as the tenant farmers prospered, so the number of landless labourers increased. The Enclosures of the18th century had already robbed them of their common land, and now those who had farmed in a very small way were forced by circumstances to give up their little plots.

In 1800 Arthur Young, the leading apostle of agricultural improvement, came across some dilapidated, but inhabited old cottages and wrote in his journal, "How very trifling the repairs to render these poor families warm and comfortable! ... What have not the great and rich people to answer, for not inquiring into the situation of their poor neighbours?"

Again, twenty years later, William Cobbett described the common condition of agricultural workers' dwellings in these terms, "Look at these hovels, made of mud and straw; bits of glass, or of old cast-off windows, without frames or hinges, but merely stuck in the mud wall ... the floor of pebble, broken brick, or the bare ground".

After a tour of England in 1851 James Caird, the leading spokesman for High Farming talked of "inconvenient, ill-arranged hovels".

These were general comments but we can assume that they would have applied to many cottages on the Rolle Estate. Indeed a visitor passing through the district in 1855, after commenting on the picturesque appearance of cob cottages in Otterton, went on to write, "There is, however, another side to the picture: cob walls when neglected lose patches from the surface, the children grub holes, and the dwellings look squalid and miserable. But when the neglect has passed into decay, and the cottage becomes a ruin, then all is picturesque again, as you will discover by numerous examples". Whatever one may think of his aesthetic sense, his reference to "numerous examples" is relevant here. Certainly there is evidence of this in Coldridge's survey of 1861, already mentioned. And in 1867 Lipscomb wrote to Mark Rolle, "It is the cottage repairs which annoy me more than any other item ... a mass of small expenditure amounting to a very large sum". Later, in 1871, he wrote again pointing out that there were about 400 cottages on the Estate which had to be kept in repair. He commented, "I am not exaggerating when I

1 & 2 Frogmore Road, East Budleigh 1879.

Brick Cottages, East Budleigh 1874.   *Cottages on the Green, Otterton 1874.*

say that 300 are in a condition which is bad both morally and in appearance, and that quite 100 should be knocked down as unworthy of repair."

Nor is it to be wondered at. A Reversionary Lease required the tenant to keep the cottage in good repair. It might have been possible for the original lessee to do so, but his successors' circumstances could well be very different. Nowadays we admire the charm of old cottages, but we can be sure that those that survive from before 1865 were the more substantial ones, those that were better built and maintained than the rest.

It appears that the last Lord Rolle only built cottages for his employees. The Trustees of his Will followed a similar policy during Mark Rolle's minority. It was therefore left to Lipscomb to push through a very extensive programme of cottage improvements in South Devon.

As early as 1877, he was able to report, "Since 1873, I have built 60 new cottages and re-roofed and thoroughly repaired 30, at a total cost of £150 apiece on the new, and £40 on those repaired . . . for bona-fide agricultural labourers only, letting the new ones at one shilling and sixpence a week". Of the new cottages, 24 were in Beer, 16 in East Budleigh, 12 in Otterton, 4 in Colaton Raleigh, 2 in Littleham and 2 in Yettington.

Although the repair of old cottages consisted mostly of re-roofing, some cob cottages, like 1 & 2 Oakhill Cottages, East Budleigh and probably 1 & 2 Frogmore Road, were extensively remodelled. In addition to re-roofing, these were raised in height and given new brick quoins and surrounds to window and door openings. The retention of the original cob walls explains the external rendering, which was not used on the new cottages.

So, to their lasting credit, Mark Rolle and Lipscomb set out from 1865 onwards to replace old dilapidated cottages with not merely better but infinitely superior ones, as the surviving examples testify.

Appendix A lists over 60 new cottages in our area built in a variety of styles or, more precisely, as variations on a common theme. As far as layout is concerned there is a strictly limited number of options.

A common plan is one having a tiny entrance lobby leading to the staircase and into a front parlour. At the back are the kitchen and pantry, while upstairs are three bedrooms. A small yard separates the back of

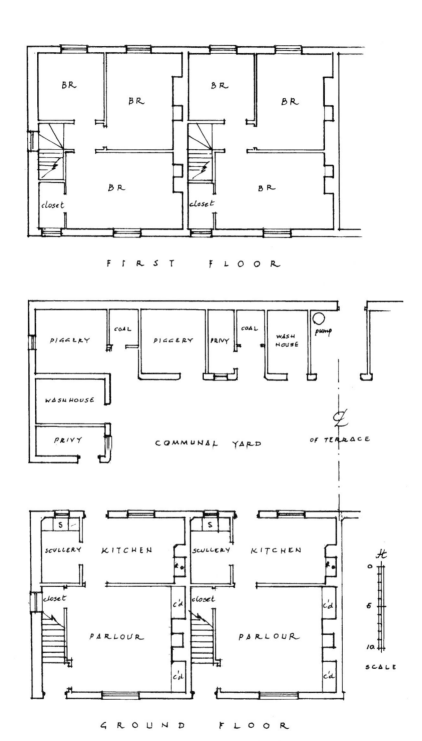

FIRST FLOOR

GROUND FLOOR

Fig 3: Plan of Cottages as built in 1877.

the cottage from the range of outbuildings which contain a privy, fuel store, washhouse and space for a pig. Such an arrangement in shown on the plan illustrated in Figure 3. It is interesting to note that the cottages were provided with a parlour (to the great benefit of the present occupants). At the time, the provision of a parlour was widely criticized as a waste of space.

How the Programme was carried through

The programme of improvements was not confined to the buildings. As we have noted, the main problem with introducing High Farming onto the Estate was the smallness of the farms.

Even before Mark Rolle's time, an attempt had been made to increase the size of individual farms by amalgamation. This process continued into his period. Nevertheless, very few farms were much over 100 acres by 1892, still very small by Caird's standards. It was not only the farms that were small; so were many of the fields, which was another hindrance to improvement. Lipscomb refers to a case where 8 fields and a lane were combined to create a field of no more than 12½ acres.

To make matters worse, some of the fields were isolated from the farms to which they belonged. Lipscomb had to arrange exchanges of land between farms to rationalize the situation.

That the attempt to increase farm sizes was not more successful was due to three factors. Firstly, there was the difficulty of repossessing farms held under Reversionary Leases. Secondly, the hilly local topography in some parts of the Estate did not lend itself to large farms. Lastly, Mark Rolle and Lipscomb lacked the necessary ruthlessness, as evidenced in a letter from Lipscomb. "I shall meet the Tenants at Otterton on Tuesday next at the Rent dinner, and be glad of your permission to tell them that no one who is farming his land tolerably and paying rent punctually will be turned out." Further reorganization would have to wait on mortality. "I am sure you do not wish to turn out anyone who has been paying rent for 50 years, but that you will be satisfied if the smaller holdings are merged with the larger ones as deaths among the tenants put them at your disposal."

That more was not done to enlarge farms may also have been because Lipscomb was not convinced of the merits of what he called "the large farm system".

Northmostown Farmhouse, Ottery Road, Newton Poppleford.

Northmostown Farm barn.

As to the building work, at first all the larger works were contracted out. Tenders were invited on the basis of plans and specifications prepared in the Estate office by Robert Kingdom, the Clerk of Works, from the time that Lipscomb took over as Steward until Kingdom's death in 1892.

Plans and specifications were sent to Mark Rolle for approval, and here Lipscomb initially ran into difficulties. Mark Rolle did not merely glance at the plans and give them the nod, as Lipscomb may not unreasonably have expected. With all the enthusiasm of a young man he studied them closely, and found much to propose by way of alteration. This earned him a rebuke from his Steward. "I am sorry that you wish for the alterations which you mention, because it is scarcely possible to meet your wishes without destroying the Plans and Specifications which have been prepared with great care and have taken up much valuable time".

On a second occasion, his frustration was even more evident. "Your letter which I have received today implies that the plans have been drawn without consideration, and you desire me to lessen the accommodation. I don't think you can believe how disheartening this is to me and to Kingdom. I have seen as much Farm Building expenditure as most Agents of my age, and Kingdom has been seeing nothing else all his life".

These early skirmishes must have made it plain to Lipscomb that Mark Rolle would not be deterred from taking an active interest in the design of properties on his Estate. In the end, the sensible solution was adopted. Rough preliminary drawings only were to be sent to Mark Rolle so that any ideas he might have could be incorporated in the finished drawings.

When Lipscomb was Steward, he had a clerk, John Millyard, to assist him in the office. There was Sharman the forester, and Philip Sanders, the Bailiff of Bicton Home Farm, but of all his assistants Robert Kingdom, the Clerk of Works for the Bicton Estate, was of the greatest importance in carrying out the extensive building work on the South Devon Estate. Kingdom was one of five Clerks of Works. There were three more in North Devon, and one at Beer, but Kingdom is by far the most important for our story.

In his 'Old Hints', Lipscomb advised the aspiring young land agent, "Over every large building job have a thoroughly competent and trustworthy man constantly on the spot in the interests of the landowner. Keep your

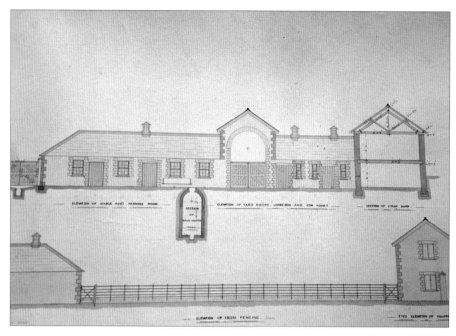

South Farm, Otterton: detail of original drawing 1869

South Farm: entrance archway

own eyes open, and your mouth shut".

On the South Devon Estate (renamed East Devon Estate from 1884), that competent and trustworthy man was Kingdom. In this Lipscomb was fortunate and knew himself to be so. At one time he described him as "a very clever fellow" even if he did add "but he is terribly prejudiced and is too old to take a hint readily!". Kingdom prepared the plans and specifications for the new buildings on the Estate. His signature is on the designs for Dotton Farm. Although he did not sign the plans for South Farm (also in the Estate Office), the style of drawing is the same. Incidentally, these latter drawings were signed by Lipscomb and Birmingham, a builder from Broadclyst who carried out several contracts for the Estate. They were presumably the contract set.

This long-serving, hard working Clerk of Works was a man after Lipscomb's own heart, well worth his £100 a year (together with a rent-free cottage and an allowance for the upkeep of a horse). Writing to Mark Rolle early in 1892, shortly before his own retirement and death, he comments with evident affection, "Dear old Kingdom's end will in all probability come suddenly – he ought to be enjoying a well-earned half-pay pension all this time, instead of which he works as a rule more than 12 hours a day".

Lipscomb's forecast was accurate, but not in the way he might have expected. "Dear old Kingdom" was returning one evening from Littleham to his home at Waterloo Cottage, Exmouth in his pony and trap, when the pony bolted and crashed into a lamppost. He was thrown out, landed on his head, and killed instantly. The accident occurred on 9 May 1892, and Kingdom was subsequently buried in All Saints Churchyard, East Budleigh. He and Lipscomb died within nine days of each other and a fruitful partnership was over.

After a few years' experience of contractors, Lipscomb decided that even the major works could be executed more efficiently and expeditiously by the Estate workforce. Outside contractors were used sparingly from then on.

The workforce that Kingdom with his assistant clerk of works (latterly his very able son Frank) had under his command was considerable. In a report to Mark Rolle in 1872, Lipscomb lists seven joiners, four carpenters, ten masons with two apprentices (who presumably also served as

Hayes Barton Farm, East Budleigh

Hayes Barton Farm

Clysthayes Farm, Knowle Road,
Budleigh Salterton

bricklayers), two painters, one plumber and his assistant, one blacksmith and a hammer man, and sixteen labourers - a total of forty-five.

Lipscomb comments on each man in turn. The quality varies from "worn out, ill, crippled and often at home" and "a rare old servant but nearly worn out. Eyesight bad" through to " a good workman but not rapid. An old soldier!", "ought to be worn out but isn't" (the man was 75) and on again to "a first rate workman", "a mason's labourer strong and active" and "a respectable trustworthy man". Somewhere in the middle of the range of ability is John Coplestone, whose age is given as 75. Of him Lipscomb writes, "Potters about Bicton Yard, sawing stones". One can just picture it!

The men's wages at this time ranged between 7 shillings a week for 18 year old labourers and 18 shillings for the top joiners and the plumber. 11 shillings was the uniform rate for the older labourers, while the average tradesman's wage was about 16 shillings. The wages had been increased by a shilling a week in 1867 but were still below the national average recorded by Baxter in that year. His "Hierarchy of Labour" shows farm labourers with an average income of 14 shillings a week, and building tradesmen earning up to twice that amount.

In reporting this labour force to Mark Rolle, Lipscomb pleaded successfully for an increase in wages but advocated that such increases should be related to the individual's capabilities and length of service. He obviously felt quite passionately about the problem of rural poverty. He commented, "I hear the farmers complain all round of the deterioration of the farm labourer, and that the day labourer's profession has become such a poor one that no young man with any "go" in him will submit to it – a bare existence and Parish Relief in old age do not hold out a very bright prospect". The comment reflects the general drift of labour from countryside to town that was taking place everywhere.

It may be that it was at Lipscomb's suggestion that Mark Rolle instituted a limited pension scheme for the workmen directly employed by the Estate. "2 shillings and sixpence to any man who has worked for 25 years on the Estate and who may become incapacitated, and he (i.e. Mark Rolle) is willing to give 7 shillings a week to old men who may get too old for regular work but who may be willing to do light jobs. Mr Rolle feels that there is a difficulty in giving pensions to old servants because the Parish will make his doing so an excuse for giving no outdoor relief." Despite

Cottages 1 - 3 South Farm Road 1905.

46 - 54 Fore Street, Otterton 1902

the Poor Law Amendment Act of 1834, which set up Union Workhouses to house, miserably, those who had previously received outdoor relief, this relief was still obtainable from the Parish where no workhouse existed, or where the authorities were reluctant to use them.

Not only did the Estate have its own substantial labour force, it also had its own means of producing much of the necessary building materials. There was a sawmill, near Sawmill Cottages, East Budleigh, deriving power from a reservoir in Yettington and converting timber from the Estate. A brick works and tilery was situated to the east of Piscombe Farm on the road between Otterton and Ladram, conveniently placed to receive coal for the kilns from Ladram Bay. There were also small brick-fields at Knowle Hill and Ting Tong, but these were let to building contractors. Flints, which were often used in the building work and for boundary walls, could readily be gathered from the fields. Even the sandstone for the buildings might have come from small quarries on the Estate such as the one in Knowle Road, Budleigh Salterton, although it is likely that it was also obtained at the larger quarry at Heavitree in Exeter.

The freestone quarries at Beer belonged to the Estate, but were let to a quarrying company. Under the terms of the lease, the Estate received royalties on all stone sent out of the quarries, in addition to obtaining stone for Estate purposes at a very favourable rate. This would have been of limited benefit, as the stone is inappropriate for plain external use, although it was used for the quoins on flint cottages at Beer where it was much cheaper than brick.

The building work dropped off markedly after Lipscomb and Kingdom had left the scene. It may well be that the most pressing needs had now been met, but there was also the realization that the Estate had become less profitable since the days when the main programme of improvements was put in hand.

Under the new Steward, Chamier, cottages were built in Colaton Raleigh in 1893, in Otterton in 1902 and in South Farm Road in 1905, in a rather different and simpler style than those built earlier.

Rolle Terrace, East Budleigh 1877.

Rolle Terrace, East Budleigh 1877.

*Old Mill House, Hayes Lane,
East Budleigh 1876.*

Finance and Falling Rents

The programme of improvements on the Estate, when hardly a year passed from 1868 to 1886 without at least two major projects being undertaken, was a remarkable achievement particularly in view of the financial constraints.

As we have noted, the expenditure of capital was strictly controlled by the Court of Chancery, to which application had to be made whenever capital was required for a new farm building or cottage. Plans, specifications and estimates had to be submitted for approval. This incurred considerable delay, much to the frustration of a man as impulsive and impatient as Lipscomb confessed himself to be.

Once the work had been completed, usually exceeding the cost approved by the Court, it had to be inspected by an independent surveyor to confirm that it had been properly done, and the final account had to be checked. This confirmation, together with the Steward's affidavit, were then sent to the Court, but it might be many months before funds were released.

Not only did this long-winded process hinder the progress of the building programme, but also the money released often fell short of what was needed. The Court would offer £100 each for cottages which, when built to the standard that Mark Rolle required, would cost at least £150. The shortfall would have to be met out of income, for the Court, prior to the Settled Land Act of 1882, would not permit the sale of leaseholds to raise capital.

The other method of financing the building work was to borrow. Initially, loans were obtained from the Inclosure Commissioners who, by this time, were channelling Government money into agricultural improvements. Later, loans were sought from Land Improvement companies on a 31 year repayment basis at 6% interest. However, the procedures for these loans were similar to those required by the Court. After a time, Lipscomb preferred the easier course of borrowing from the bank.

The Settled Land Act of 1882 improved the situation to some degree as far as the Court of Chancery was concerned. It allowed Mark Rolle to draw on a lump sum of capital each year for projects of his own choosing without prior approval from the Court. The expenditure had, of course, to be accounted for and certified subsequently. Also, and more

Pinn Barton Cottages, Pinn Lane, Otterton 1877.

Pinn Barton Cottages.

Cross Tree Cottages, Otterton 1876.

importantly, it allowed a tenant for life, like Mark Rolle, for the first time, to sell part (or all) of the family landed estate, provided that the sales money remained subject to the family settlement. If he so wished, he could use the money to pay for improvements on the Estate.

We have already remarked that the smallness of the farms on the Estate made large investments unprofitable. As for the cottages, as an investment they were in Lipscomb's own words "a dead loss". Built at a cost of at least £150, and let for less than £4 a year, one can readily see why.

It was a tragedy for the Estate that the bulk of the improvements was put in hand at a time when the so-called Golden Age was coming to an end. The downturn in agricultural prosperity generally was becoming evident. Even as early as 1871, Lipscomb had to report, "Every man in arrears has been pushed to the utmost, without resorting to legal proceedings." In the years that followed, there are frequent references in the Steward's letter books to concessions of rent and the writing off of irrecoverable arrears. The picture is a bleak one.

Mark Rolle and Lipscomb did all they could "to keep 400 tenant farmers on their legs during such times as we have been going through", as Lipscomb puts it. In 1879 and 1880, Mark Rolle voluntarily reduced rents by 20% in a desire "to do what is just and right by his tenants if bad times continue" - which they did! His liberal action was not appreciated by other Devon landowners who, through shortage of funds or lack of generosity, could not follow his example.

By 1882, Lipscomb had come to the conclusion that a widespread revaluation of rentals on the "clay farms" was a necessity. He knew that most of the tenants could only pay by borrowing, or selling stock, which was no lasting solution. The revaluation met with a mixed reception from the tenants. Lipscomb reported that some gave "thanks and blessings", some accepted "somewhat ungraciously", others asked for more, and one was "within an inch of being insulting", illustrating the strain that the depression imposed on the relationship between landlord and tenant. Lipscomb also did his best to encourage the tenants to change their farming methods to combat the depression. He strongly advised them to lay down more fields to grass, so that they could run more cattle and reduce their dependence on no longer profitable corn crops. "Stock and butter are now the rent-makers".

Quashbrook Cottages, Church Road, Colaton Raleigh 1891.

Hayeswood Cottage, off Hayes Lane, East Budleigh 1881.

Nothing however could radically alter a situation which was beyond the control of landlord and tenant alike. Profitability for both continued to decline throughout the rest of the century and beyond.

By 1887, arrears of rent on the South Devon Estate amounted to the large sum of £3,000, and Lipscomb was advising Mark Rolle to use his capital in housing developments in towns like Exmouth. Ground rents from houses were a more reliable source of income than farm rents.

In January 1892, with Lipscomb nearly at the end of his time as Steward, he was compelled to write letters in identical terms to several of the more prominent tenant farmers. "I am well aware of the difficulties you had to contend with last harvest with your crops, but I am obliged to ask you to let me have as much rent as you can pay on account (even if you cannot pay it all) on or before 30th inst."

The growing seriousness of the financial situation from about 1870 onwards could only be ameliorated by economies. That much must have been obvious to a Steward as shrewd as Lipscomb and equally clear to Mark Rolle. Why then did they continue with the costly programme of improvements? One can only conclude that Mark Rolle, having inherited a property in a deplorable state of dereliction, felt compelled to "do right by the land" and to improve the livelihood of the tenant farmers and labourers on his Estate partly, perhaps, as a matter of prestige, but certainly with the acceptance of what he conceived to be an imperative moral duty; notwithstanding that he grew dismayed at the growing expense.

South Farm, Otterton 1869: entrance archway with Rolle Arms in roundel.

ARCHITECTURAL DESIGN

The surviving Mark Rolle buildings can be identified from certain characteristic architectural features. Once alerted to these, anyone exploring the Lower Otter Valley soon begins to recognize them as one recognizes an old friend. Although the farm buildings show only subtle differences from those that preceded them, the cottages, particularly those of the peak period, have a delightful exuberance of variety and elaboration.

The chief feature which characterizes some, but by no means all of the buildings, is the incorporation of a stone inscribed with the bold initials MR and the date of erection either on the same stone, or on a separate one. This was Mark Rolle's idea. It was apparently first used in 1863 on buildings at the Home Farm, Bicton, although here the full initials MGKR were displayed. However, this form of identification calls for a word of caution in case we assume too much from it. For example, the MR stone at Lower Pinn Farm dated 1881 can only apply to a very small part of the whole complex. Similarly at Weeks Farm in Pinn Lane, the date of 1869 in the gable of the north range only applies to that range, which even so incorporated an existing stable. In other cases, the initials may refer to a building having been repaired rather than newly built. Dotton Farm and South Farm are distinguished by the addition of the Rolle Coat of Arms within a roundel, a feature used also in North Devon but taking a different form.

Apart from the presence of a "signature" stone, the best evidence for an MR identification is the presence of distinctive corbels at the gables. These moulded brick corbels, which occur on virtually all the farm buildings and on several of the dwellings, are certainly very unusual. Corbels that project from the flank wall on the same plane as the gable are common enough, but corbels, such as these, which project at right angles to the gable and support a deeply overhanging roof verge are not. Seldom too do brick corbels comprise so many courses. If one feature can be said to be the surest pointer to a Mark Rolle provenance, it is these corbels. A full-size drawing exists in the Estate archives, although this is more elaborate than those commonly built.

Typical King-post truss at Northmostown Farm.

Detail of openings at Pitson Farm.

*Flint and brick dressings at
Flint Cottages, Otterton.*

Farm Buildings

A surprising feature of the robust architecture of the farm buildings as a whole is the variety of walling materials; red bricks from the Estate brickworks, stone and flint, very often used together. At Dotton Farm, built from scratch as we have seen, all three materials were used. And it would seem that this was done not for any specific practical purpose, but just for the appearance of it.

Pebbles were also extensively used, mostly for free-standing walls but sometimes, as at Goosemoor and Dalditch Farms, to face the buildings.

Where stone and flint were used, the quoins are of brick of the traditional bull-nosed form to lessen the risk of injury to animals or carts. The openings have brick surrounds with very flat segmental brick arches at the head. The horizontal joints in these arches are often false, merely scratched into the brick. The cills are Delabole slate. Whatever the size of the opening, the brick dressings were of a uniform size, which gives the smaller openings an engagingly self-important air. Brick walling was laid in Flemish Bond set in the strong lias lime that Kingdom favoured.

The roofs were covered either with Delabole slates or with clay tiles from the Estate tile works. Many have now been re-covered and, in the case of the tiled roofs, something of interest may have been lost. The barn at Pitson's Farm still retains its original roof covering, where bands of plain tiles alternate with bands of scalloped tiles. This feature is repeated on the stables at the rear. It can also be seen on the cottages at the north end of Castle Lane, where happily it was reproduced when one of the cottages was re-roofed recently. Some use was also made of pantiles where roof pitches were lower than normal.

The standard form of roof truss was a modified king-post truss where an iron rod replaces the conventional timber king post. The wood for the roof trusses and other substantial building timbers was usually elm, oak being in short supply on the Estate. For joinery work, deal was used. Kingdom specified pitch pine, and was much preoccupied with preventing builders from using the inferior Swedish red spruce instead. The timber was converted in the new sawmill near Sawmill Reservoir in Yettington. Lipscomb delightedly claimed that great savings had been made by the Estate having its own sawmill.

Many of the farm buildings have now, of course, been converted into

Pebbles, brick dressings & pantiles at Dalditch Farm.

Corbel at Pavers Farm.

Detail at Cottages on the Green, Otterton

dwellings or, as at South Farm, into commercial units. In a few unfortunate cases, the original character has been lost but, for the most part, the conversions have been carried out with considerable sensitivity.

Cottages

Some originality can be claimed for the design of the cottages, for they show an amazing variety, not so much in the plan form, for here the options are very limited, but in the treatment of the elevations. Of course, Kingdom, the Clerk of Works who designed these cottages, could have had the benefit of numerous sample designs, ranging from the sophisticated (and expensive) designs published earlier in the 19th century by architects such as J. B. Papworth and Francis Goodwin, to the more mundane designs illustrated in the widely-read periodical "The Builder", much the more likely source.

Nevertheless, whereas many of the large landed estates went in for a standard cottage design, often painted in the Estate colours (such as the yellow of the Cowdray Estate in Sussex), here on the Rolle Estate each pair or terrace of cottages differs in some significant way from the next.

The earliest of the dated cottages are the pair at Tidwell Barton (1868). These are built of stone with brick dressings. The numerous cottages built in the 1870s are mainly of red brick from the Estate brickworks. Often contrasting buff bricks are used, for example at the quoins and jambs of the openings, or alternating with red bricks in the window arches. These arches are very flat, hardly rising from the horizontal (and sometimes with a completely horizontal extrados), but the bricks radiate as in a true arch. Usually there is a stone springer at each end, and often a central keystone.

Most of the cottages of this earlier period have a three brick string course at the first floor level, and sometimes these are emphasized by setting bricks diagonally in the middle course of the three. Another feature is the use of burnt headers to form patterns in the brickwork, usually in the form of lozenges, although at Sawmill Cottages (now Old Mill House), for example, they are in the form of bold crosses. They are also to be seen in some of the string courses. The exceptions to the brick cottages of the 1870s are the pairs of flint cottages in Yettington (1874) and Otterton (1875). These are built of knapped flint with red brick dressings and lozenges of red brick set in the flint work. It might be thought that these pairs of cottages, built of the same materials at about the same time,

Brick details at Old Mill House, East Budleigh.

Yard at Rolle Cottages, East Budleigh.

Windows at Quashbrook Cottages, Colaton Raleigh.

would be identical, but this is not so. It would be tedious to detail all the, slight, differences, but it demonstrates how the Estate eschewed uniformity.

As the rooms in the upper stories were partly in the roof space, small gablets were introduced above the principal windows, which give liveliness to the facades. The roofs were generally tiled and surmounted with trefoil-crested ridge tiles. These have not always been retained when the roofs were re-tiled.

The characteristic windows in these earlier cottages are distinctive. With the exception of those at Tidwell Barton, they are mullioned, with transoms usually on the ground floor only. The casements are divided into panes of horizontal proportions, in contrast to the traditional Georgian vertical pane. It is interesting to note however that, where farmhouses were newly built, the Georgian proportions were used for the windows, perhaps to make a class distinction between the farmer and his labourers!

With the departure of both Lipscomb and Kingdom in 1892, a distinct change is apparent in the design of the later cottages. Not only are they simpler, but also several of them were rendered when built (whereas the rendering on a few of the earlier cottages most likely indicates that they were originally old cob cottages that were extensively repaired and improved). The roofs are more often slated than tiled, and the panes of the casements have reverted to Georgian proportions. Moreover, rather strangely, most of these later cottages have the distinctive moulded corbels. Although, as we have seen, these were used on nearly all the farm buildings, they are absent from all the earlier cottages apart from the flint cottages and a few outbuildings. The cottages at 46 to 54 Fore Street, Otterton (1902) and those in South Farm Road (1905) have projecting pitched hoods, supported on curved brackets, over the doors. The only other occurrence of this feature in this form is on the cottages ("Otter Rise") at the entrance to South Farm. It is tempting to think that the Otter Rise hoods were added at the same time as the cottages were rendered, and the roofs re-covered in slate.

Figure 3 (page 54) shows the plan of a typical row of cottages, including the range of outbuildings separated from the rear of the cottages by a narrow continuous yard. This acted as a common thoroughfare, and

Pavers Farm, Ottery Road, Otterton.

Dotton Farm 1871.

*Dalditch Farm, Dalditch Lane,
East Budleigh.*

gave access to the communal pump. The outbuildings housed a
wash-house, a fuel store, a privy and usually a pig sty, for each cottage.
Generally they were built in the same style as the cottages but, more
often than not, the roofs were covered with clay pantiles.

Sir Henry Wotton (1568-1639) wrote "Well building hath three conditions:
Commodity, Firmness and Delight", or, as we might now say, "Utility,
Stability and Delight". Judged on these criteria, the buildings of the Mark
Rolle era are unquestionably outstanding examples of "Well-building".

Hill Farm, East Budleigh 1890/91.

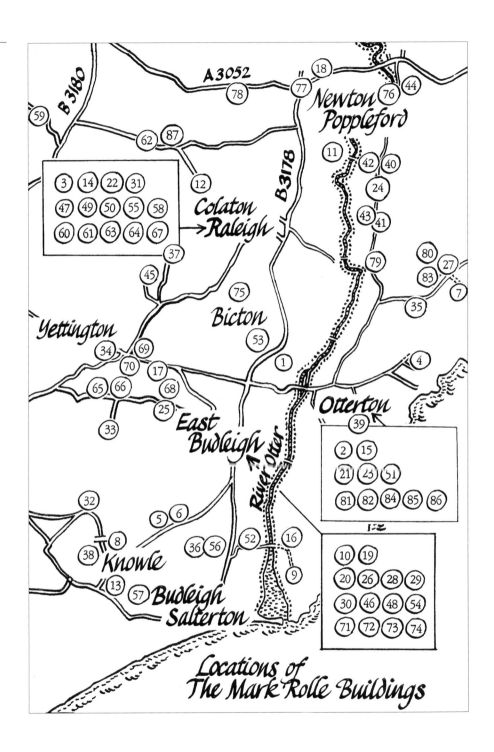

Locations of
The Mark Rolle Buildings

CONCLUSION

The buildings we have been looking at are the remains of a social and economic order that is past. Great landowners, like Mark Rolle, had the power to change the built environment on their estates and, indeed, to some extent the agricultural pattern also. Even in Mark Rolle's lifetime, their control over the countryside was beginning to wane, but it is important to remember that, although they exercised great sway over the locality and its community, they were themselves a part of that community. Where they were benevolent, like Mark Rolle, that benevolence was personal. They were not faceless.

At the end of our survey, it becomes clear that the scheme of improvements on the Estate had more to do with human values than with maximising profits. Mark Rolle's approach to the modernization of his property was essentially paternalistic in the best sense of that word.

Neither Mark Rolle nor Lipscomb could have deluded themselves that financial benefit would accrue from the massive programme of work. Indeed, as Lipscomb pointed out to his chief as early as 1871, the income Mark Rolle derived from the Estate could be increased by some £4,000 per annum (or about 25%) if the programme were to be abandoned. Obviously, this idea did not appeal to Mark Rolle. One suspects that Lipscomb knew that would be the case.

In 1874, he wrote to his chief, "I am not at all surprised at the state of finances you describe knowing, as I do, how liberal and generous you are, and I am sure that no one realizes more than I do how very little you get out of the property. I have often said that it was not worth all the trouble and annoyance which it gives you". But we may be thankful that Mark Rolle did not see it that way!

On the Rolle Estate, an architectural legacy was left to us that merits our admiration and protection. Indeed, the legacy might well serve as an example to us. The use of local materials, the inventiveness, the variety and the element of fun, which stops short of whimsicality; these are qualities well worth striving to emulate in the buildings of today.

THE BUILDINGS

Buildings in the five parishes identified as built, added to or altered during the time of Mark Rolle

BS - Budleigh Salterton, CR – Colaton Raleigh, EB – East Budleigh,
NP – Newton Poppleford, O – Otterton
Note: The boundary between Newton Poppleford and Otterton has been moved since Mark Rolle's time. The following list refers to the modern parishes.

	BUILDINGS MARKED "MR" AND DATED	Date	Map ref:
1	Bicton College Farm, EB (original Home Farm)	1863	0765 8570
2	Rolle Barton (part), Church Hill, O (converted)	1867	0790 8506
3	Pophams Farm (part)	1868	0715 8780
4	Seaview Farm, O	1868	0952 8568
5	Tidwell Barton Cottages, EB (now combined) and	1868	0602 8331
6	Tidwell Barton Farm, EB (built at the same time)	1868	0608 8333
7	Weeks Farm (part), Pinn Lane, O	1869	1028 8678
8	Higher Knowle Farm, BS (converted)	1869	0499 8291
9	South Farm, O (converted)	1869	0780 8275
10	Pulhayes Farm, EB	1870	0705 8405
11	Dotton Farm, CR	1871	0845 8860
12	Kingston Farm (part), Stowford Hill, CR	1873	0652 8782
13	Rolle Cottages, Village Street, Knowle, BS	1873	0505 8265
14	Popham's Farm Cottages, CR	1874	0718 8775
15	Cottages on The Green, O	1874	0805 8527
16	Cottages at entrance to South Farm, O	1874	0768 8305
17	Flint Cottages, Yettington, EB	1874	0564 8568
18	Langsford Farm, NP (converted)	1874	0823 8962
19	Cottages, 3 & 4 Middle Street, EB	1874	0665 8448
20	Cottages, 1 & 2 Middle Street, EB	1875	0665 8448
21	Flint Cottages, Ottery Street, O	1875	0842 8542
22	Greenhill Cottages, behind church, CR	1875	0817 8708
23	Cottages at Cross Tree Farm, Lea Road, O	1876	0842 8531
24	Houghton Farm (part), NP	1876	0905 8818

25	Sawmill Cottages, Hayes Lane, EB (now combined as Old Mill House)	1876	0586 8505
26	Rolle Cottages, Budleigh Hill, EB	1877	0694 8425
27	Pinn Barton Cottages, Pinn Lane, O	1877	1012 8686
28	Cottages, 1 & 2 Oakhill, EB	1878	0695 8448
29	Cottages, 1 & 2 Frogmore Road, EB	1879	0699 8437
30	Wynhay House, EB (converted)	1879	0661 8460
31	Hardy's Farm, Hawkerland Road, CR	1879	0758 8769
32	Dalditch Farm (part), Dalditch Lane, EB	1879	0473 8360
33	Hayeswood Cottage, off Hayes Lane, EB	1881	0508 8471
34	Lufflands Farm (part), Yettington, EB (converted)	1881	0535 8575
35	Lower Pinn Farm (part), Pinn Lane, O	1881	0965 8650

(Note: This Farmhouse and most of buildings date from 1864)

36	Kersbrook Farm (part), BS	1882	0655 8305
37	Stowford Farm, CR	1884	0608 8716
38	Knowle House (cowhouse/piggery), Dalditch Lane, BS	1884	0469 8282
39	Stantyway Farm (stables), Stantyway Cross, O	1885	0888 8490
40	Pitson Farm (part), Ottery Road, NP	1885	0913 8847
41	Passaford Farm (part), Ottery Road, O	1886	0907 8765
42	Ashtree Farm (outbuilding), Ottery Road, NP	1886	0904 8848
43	Pavers Farm (part), Ottery Road, O	1886	0900 8767
44	Northmostown Farm (detached buildings, dated) NP	1886	0936 8945
45	Stowford House (small addition), CR	1886	0560 8677
46	Hill Farm, Hayes Lane, EB (converted)	1890	0648 8489
47	Quashbrook Cottages, Church Road, CR	1891	0779 8750
48	Syon Barn, Frogmore Road, EB	1893	0724 8445
49	Baileys Cottages, Church Road, CR	1893	0789 8746
50	Old School House & Barley Mow, Church Road, CR	1893	0816 8718
51	Cottages, 46 to 54 Fore Street, O	1902	0820 8526
52	Cottages, 1 to 3 South Farm Road, EB	1905	0700 8302

OTHER DATED FEATURES

| 53 | Shell House, Bicton Gardens, EB | 1845 | 0742 8590 |

(Note: Mark Rolle, aged 10, and Lady Louisa Rolle)

| 54 | Main water tap point, EB | 1887 | 0667 8461 |
| 55 | Main water tap point, CR | 1887 | 0776 8749 |

UNDATED BUILDINGS   Map ref:

56 Mill House, Kersbrook, BS (altered 1868, new roof,   0652 8306
     windows and outbuildings added)

57 Clysthayes Farm barns, Knowle Road, BS (converted)   0558 8229

58 Old Forge, Hawkerland Road, CR   0770 8763

59 Stallcombe House, Sanctuary Lane, CR ("MR" stone 1884   0386 8910
     and roundhouse transferred from farm in Woodbury)

60 Plewlands, Hawkerland Road, CR (converted)   0758 8769

61 No. 2 Hardy's Cottages, CR (once part of Hardy's Farm)   0749 8768

62 Valley Barn, Hawkerland Road, CR (converted)   0561 8870

63 Blue Ball Dairy, Main Road, CR (buildings at rear and in   0773 8746
     adjoining yard – formerly part of Drupe Farm)

64 Drupe Farm except farmhouse, Main Road, CR (conv)   0765 8720

65 Hayes Barton Farm, Hayes Lane, EB (buildings by house) 0505 8522

66 Hayes Barton Farm, Hayes Lane, EB (buildings by road) 0507 8514
     (Note: Great barn is possibly pre-Mark Rolle)

67 Cottage at right angles to Main Road, Colaton Cross, CR   0774 8756

68 Old Sawmill, Yettington, EB   0590 8516

69 Lemprice Farm, Yettington, EB   0548 8560

70 Sandycross Farm, Yettington, EB (minor repairs only)   0540 8569

71 Syon House, EB (probably built 1840s, outbuildings later)   0712 8453

72 Cottages, 1 to 3 Budleigh Hill, EB (re-roofing)   0696 8435

73 Wynards House, High Street, EB (buildings at rear)   0659 8471

74 Wynards Farm (part), Middle Street, EB   0658 8462

75 Keepers Cottage, Bicton College, EB   0705 8665

76 Smith's Farm, Ottery Road, NP (outbuilding)   0926 8940

77 Langsford Barns, A3052, NP   0790 8950

78 Goosemoor Farm, A 3052, NP   0700 8951

79 Burnthouse Farm, Ottery Road, O (small shed)   0898 8702

80 Horstone, Pinn Lane, O (outbuilding)   1018 8693

81 Houstern Farm, Fore Street, O (barn)   0824 8526

82 Homestone, Fore Street, O   0828 8528
     (buildings, formerly part of Watering Farm)

83 Pinn Barton, Pinn Lane, O (implement shed)   1003 8692

84 Cottages, 10 to 24, Ottery Street, O (re-roofing only?)   0845 8540

85 Cottages, 66 to 68 Fore Street, O (re-roofing only?)   0821 8528

86 Anchoring Farm except farmhouse, Ottery Street, O   0848 8550
     (converted)

87 Hawkerland Chapel, CR (converted)   0597 8869

NOTES

1   The inclusion of several of the undated buildings is to some
     extent speculative. The sheer scale of the building operations
     and, in particular, the frequent references in the letter books to
     repairs suggest that several buildings have yet to be identified.
2   Many dwellings were built on Estate land in Budleigh Salterton
     (and Exmouth) on building leases. Although the designs had to
     be approved by the Estate and the builders had to adhere to its
     specifications, these houses cannot be classed as Estate buildings
     and are not listed here.

Appendix B

THE ESTATES NOW

Although much of the Estate land in North Devon around Torrington was
sold in the 20th century, what remains, now known as the Clinton Devon
Estates, still runs to over 23,000 acres.

The large Clinton Estate in the Lower Otter Valley, stretching out eastward
towards Mutters Moor and westward to beyond Woodbury, is the main
holding. Further east is the small Beer Estate. In North Devon, the
Heanton Estate, centred on Merton, runs alongside the River Torridge.

The Estates include 80% of East Devon's rare Pebblebed Heaths, over
2,800 acres of which are accessible to the public. There are about 4,600
acres of woodland, where a deliberate policy of bio-diversity is pursued.
Over 4,500 acres are farmed with a mixture of arable, dairy and livestock
farming. There are 40 tenant farmers managing farms of between 150
and 500 acres, so the farms, as in Mark Rolle's day, are still comparatively
small. What is different is the high proportion of Home Farms.

There are still numerous farm buildings and cottages on the Estates,
though none of the derelict buildings that confronted Mark Rolle's
Stewards. The burden of maintenance on so large a scale is obvious, and
we are fortunate to have Lord Clinton and his staff to protect this valuable
feature of our built environment

GLOSSARY

CASEMENT: a hinged or pivoted window

CORBEL: a projecting block of stone, brick or wood, often moulded, which projects from a wall to support a beam or other feature

DRESSINGS: stone or brick surrounds (including the jambs) around an opening or other feature, and at the quoins, to give emphasis

EXTRADOS: the line formed by the outer edge of an arch

HEADER: a brick laid so that only the end appears on the face of a wall

JAMB: stone or brickwork forming the vertical surround to a door or window opening

KEYSTONE: the central stone in an arch

KING-POST: the central vertical post in a king-post truss

LOZENGE: a diamond shape

MULLION: a main vertical member dividing a window opening

QUOIN: stone or brickwork used at the external corners of a building

SPRINGER: a stone forming the sloping abutment at each end of an arch

STRING COURSE: a continuous horizontal band of brick or stone, either plain or moulded, and usually projecting from the face of a building

TRANSOM: a main horizontal intermediate member dividing a window opening

BIBLIOGRAPHY

AUSTIN, Anne:	*History of the Clinton Barony*	1999
BAGLEY, J. J. and A. J.:	*The English Poor Law*	1966
BEST, Geoffrey:	*Mid-Victorian Britain 1851-75*	1979
BRIGDEN, Roy:	*Victorian Farms*	1986
BROOMHALL, W. (ed.):	*The Country Gentlemen's Estate Book*	1902
BROWN, Robert:	*The Book of the Landed Estate*	1869
CHERRY, Bridget & PEVSNER, Nikolaus:	*The Buildings of England: Devon*	1989
GREY, Todd (ed.):	*The Travellers Tales, Vol.2: East Devon*	2000
HARVEY, Nigel:	*Old Farm Buildings*	1975
LAUDER, R. A. :	*Vanished Houses of North Devon*	1981
LIPSCOMB, R. H.:	*Old Hints for Young Land Agents, Chapter 38, Walmesley's Rural Estate Management, 5th edition*	*1969*
MATHIAS, Peter:	*The First Industrial Nation: An Economical History of Britain 1700-1914*	1969
MINGAY, G. E.:	*Rural Life in Victorian England*	1977
OTTER VALLEY ASSOCIATION:	*Historical Guide to the Lower Otter Valley*	1984
PARKER, M. St. J & REID, D. J.:	*The British Revolution 1750-1970. A Social and Economic History*	1972
PERREN, Richard:	*Agriculture in Depression 1870-1940*	1995
ROBINSON, John Martin:	*The English Country Estate*	1988
SPRING, David:	*The English Landed Estate in the Nineteenth Century: Its Administration*	1963
TREVELYAN, G. M.:	*English Social History*	1944
WILSON, John:	*British Farming*	1862

OTHER SOURCES

ROLLE ESTATE ARCHIVES, Syon House, East Budleigh
DEVON RECORDS OFFICE, Exeter
WEST COUNTRY STUDIES, Exeter
TORRINGTON MUSEUM, Great Torrington
FAIRLYNCH MUSEUM, Budleigh Salterton

The Hon. Mark Rolle in later years.

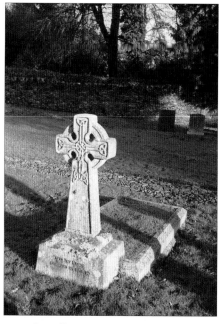

Mark Rolle's grave at Huish Church,
North Devon.